T is for Touchdown

A Football Alphabet

Written by Brad Herzog and Illustrated by Mark Braught

Photo reference used on the R page: courtesy of Tournament of Roses Archives.

Sleeping Bear Press™

315 E. Eisenhower Parkway, Ste. 200
Ann Arbor, MI 48108
www.sleepingbearpress.com

Sleeping Bear Press, a part of Cengage Learning.

10 9 8 7 6 5 4 (case)
10 9 8 7 6 5 (pbk)

Library of Congress Cataloging-in-Publication Data

Herzog, Brad.
T is for touchdown : a football alphabet / written by Brad Herzog;
illustrated by Mark Braught.
p. cm.

pbk ISBN-13: 978-1-58536-337-7   **case** ISBN-13: 978-1-58536-233-2

1. Football—Juvenile literature. 2. Alphabet books—Juvenile literature.
I. Braught, Mark, ill. II. Title.
GV950.7.H47 2004
797.332—dc22   2004006108
Printed by China Translation & Printing Services Limited,
Guangdong Province,China. 5th printing . 06/2012

To Bernard "Bunny" Rosenblum, captain of the 1916
New Castle (Pennsylvania) High football team.

BRAD

∾

For all the members, staff, and volunteers of the Boys & Girls Clubs of America
and the communities, corporations, and individuals that support them and
the important work they do for our future. Thank you.

MARK

A is for amazing athletes
who always aim to win—
        the A-number-one football stars
        picked All-American.

The first All-American football team appeared in 1889, when magazine owner Caspar Whitney decided to list the 11 college football players who were best at their positions. Since then, many different organizations have chosen All-Americans for both high school and college football.

A is also for the Arena Football League (AFL), which features football played indoors on a field 50 yards long. Each team lines up eight players, and most of them compete on both offense and defense. It is an exciting brand of football. Players bounce off padded sideline barriers, and the ball bounces off nets just beyond the end zone. Teams often combine for more than 100 points in a game. The AFL has brought pro football to smaller cities, such as Peoria, Illinois. Former AFL quarterback Kurt Warner became a two-time Most Valuable Player in the National Football League.

A
a

The football, an inflated oval with laces, is often called a pigskin. But most modern footballs are made from cowhide leather or (for younger players) rubber. Pro football uses a slightly larger ball (11 to 11½ inches long and 14 to 15 ounces in weight) than the college game. In general, the football increases in size as the people throwing it grow.

Early footballs were larger, rounder, and difficult to throw. But as the football began to take on its modern shape, the forward pass became a vital part of the game. A perfectly thrown pass is called a spiral. It is thrown by placing your index finger (pointer) at the beginning of the laces, then putting the rest of your fingers in every other lace and your thumb around the back of the football. Bring the football to ear level, rotate your hips and try to make your fingers be the last thing to touch the ball.

B b

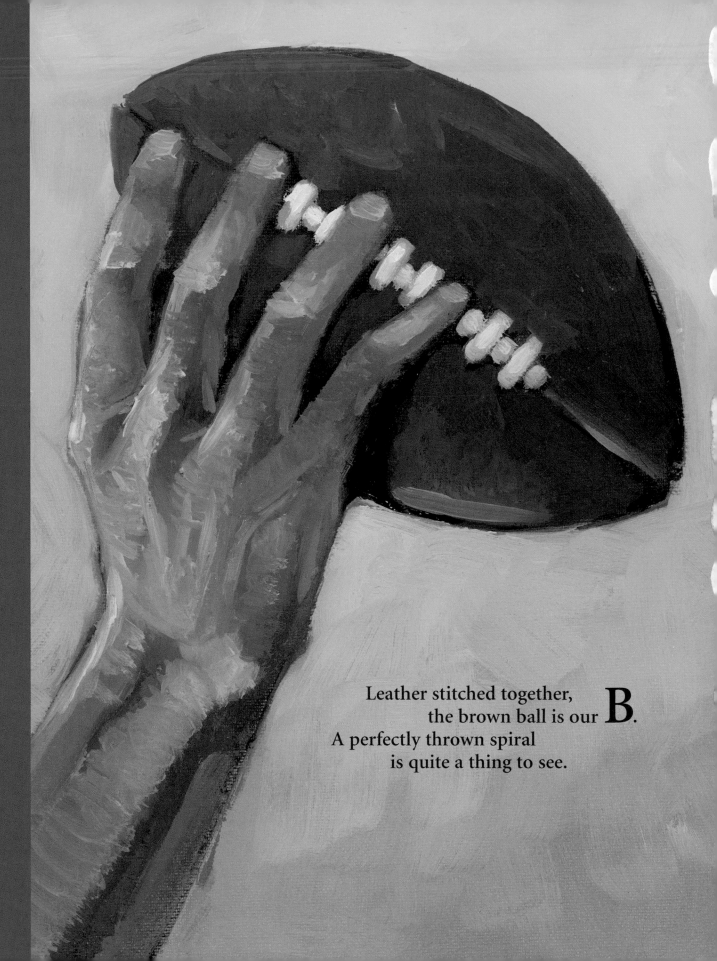

Leather stitched together,
the brown ball is our B.
A perfectly thrown spiral
is quite a thing to see.

Canton, Ohio—that's the C that cradled the pro game. The city is now home to the Pro Football Hall of Fame.

The Ohio city of Canton was chosen as the site of the Pro Football Hall of Fame because it was there that the National Football League was founded in 1920. Since the Hall of Fame opened in 1963, more than 200 players, coaches, and contributors have been inducted. The building houses hundreds of historical displays in 51,000 square feet of space.

The first recorded instance of a game resembling modern North American football took place between a Canadian team (McGill University) and an American squad (Harvard University) in 1874. Today, many American college football stars go on to play professionally in the Canadian Football League (CFL). There are several important differences between Canadian and American pro football. The CFL uses a slightly rounder ball, a longer and wider field, three downs to gain 10 yards instead of four, and 12 instead of 11 players per side. The league's championship game is known as the Grey Cup.

Usually, four defensive linemen, three line-backers, and four players in the secondary make up the defense. Linemen try to tackle the ball carrier on running plays and rush the quarterback on passing plays. Linebackers usually stand a few yards behind the linemen to guard against a run or pass. The secondary (or defensive backfield) includes two corner-backs and two safeties who guard against a long pass. They may play man-to-man defense (each player covers a particular receiver) or zone defense (each player covers an area of the field).

The offense has four downs (plays) in which to gain at least 10 yards. The first try is called first-and-10, meaning it is the first down and the team is 10 yards away from making another first down. If the team gains three yards, then the next play is second-and-7, and so on. On fourth down, a team may either punt the ball down the field or "go for it," trying to gain a first down. If they don't make it, the other team takes over where the play stopped.

D is for the defense,
refusing to give ground
and stopping the opposing team
from making a first down.

E is also for end zone, a rectangular area that is 10 yards deep on most football fields. At the back of the end zone are goalposts connected by a horizontal crossbar 10 feet off the ground. The goalposts (also called uprights) are 18½ feet apart.

After a team scores a touchdown, achieved by reaching the end zone, it may attempt an extra point conversion. Usually, a place-kicker tries for one point (a PAT, or point after touchdown). The ball is placed on the two-yard line (three-yard line in college and high school) and snapped to a holder, who places it on its tip. The kicker must kick the ball over the crossbar and through the goal-posts. However, teams may also try for two points by running or passing the ball into the end zone from the three-yard line.

E is eleven players to a side, too. A penalty may be called if too many or too few players are on the field.

E is for an extra point
kicked straight through the goalposts.
When trying to eke out a win,
one point can matter most.

A fumble occurs when a ball carrier drops the football before he is tackled. An offensive or defensive player may recover a fumble and run with it until tackled.

F is also for flag football. Defenders "tackle" opposing players by simply grabbing one of two flags hanging from a belt around the ball carrier's waist. Because there is no actual tackling, it is a safer version of football. In touch football, another popular form of the game, a play is over when a defender touches the ball carrier with one or two hands (local rules decide).

Another **F** is Doug Flutie. Standing only 5-foot-10 (quite short for a pro quarterback), he became perhaps the best player in Canadian Football League history. In his eight-year CFL career he won six Most Outstanding Player awards. Flutie also won the 1984 Heisman Trophy as the outstanding college player and was still playing in the National Football League at age 41.

F is for a failure
to hold onto the ball.
When finally the pile clears,
fumble is the call.

G is for graceful Red Grange.
      They called him "Galloping Ghost."
He gave the game a great big lift
      by playing coast-to-coast.

G g

Harold "Red" Grange was called "The Galloping Ghost" because he was so hard to catch. After starring for the University of Illinois, he became the first college standout to turn professional, joining the Chicago Bears of the then five-year-old National Football League in 1925. Pro football wasn't very popular yet, but Grange played 19 games in 17 cities over 66 days. Huge crowds watched and gained an appreciation for the pro game.

G is also for gridiron, which is what many people call a football field. The name comes from the fact that someone once thought the yard lines on the field made it resemble an iron cooking griddle. The field, which is 100 yards long and 53½ yards wide, is marked with solid white lines every five yards and yard numbers every 10 yards. Each yard is marked by a short white line called a hash mark. Coaches and substitute players stand on the sidelines, which are out-of-bounds.

Huddle up for **H** now.
The head coach called a play—
a handoff to the halfback,
who might go all the way.

H
h

"Hut... hut... hike!" is the way many people call for the ball to be snapped when they are beginning a play. A play does not begin until the center snaps or hikes the ball, handing or tossing it through his legs to the quarterback.

H is also for Heisman Trophy, which is awarded each year to the outstanding college football player in the nation. The award, named after former Georgia Tech University coach John Heisman, has been presented since 1935. Ohio State University running back Archie Griffin is the only man to win the trophy twice.

H is for high school football, too. Over one million boys and some 3,000 girls compete in high school football on more than 14,000 teams each year. Small schools with fewer than 100 students play a form of the game known as eight-man football, which features three fewer players on each side and is played on an 80-yard field.

When a defensive player catches a pass intended for a receiver, he may run the interception back until he is tackled. James Willis \of the Philadelphia Eagles holds the NFL record for the longest interception return— 104 yards, from one end zone to the other.

I is also for inches. Football is often called "a game of inches" because a few inches can make all the difference. A ball carrier can be tackled inches short of the goal line, for instance, or a receiver can be just inches short of catching a long pass. It is common for teams to be very close to achieving a first down. When that happens, members of the "chain gang" are asked to measure exactly. They carry a 10-foot yardage chain onto the field to determine exactly where the first down line is. The players on both sides watch eagerly, and the crowd holds its breath. Is the ball beyond the 10-yard mark? Yes! First down!

I is for an interception,
when a thrown pass lands
where the passer didn't aim—
his opponent's hands.

Ii

J is for the jerseys—
names and numbers, too.
Despite the football helmets,
we can tell who is who.

J j

NFL rules require that certain players wear certain numbers on their jerseys. In general, quarterbacks and kickers wear numbers 1 to 19, running backs and defensive backs wear 20 to 49, centers and linebackers wear 50 to 59, defensive and offensive tackles and guards wear 60 to 79, wide receivers and tight ends wear 80 to 89, and defensive ends wear 90 to 99. Which numbers have been worn by the most Pro Football Hall of Famers? Numbers 16 and 44.

Football can be rough, so players wear protective equipment from head to toe. Most important is the helmet, which protects the head and is held securely by a chin strap. To protect the face, face masks, which resemble cages with horizontal bars, are attached to the helmet. Players often protect their teeth with mouth guards, as well. Padding is also worn beneath the uniform, including shoulder pads, hip pads, and thigh pads. Cleated shoes help football players maintain their footing.

k

K

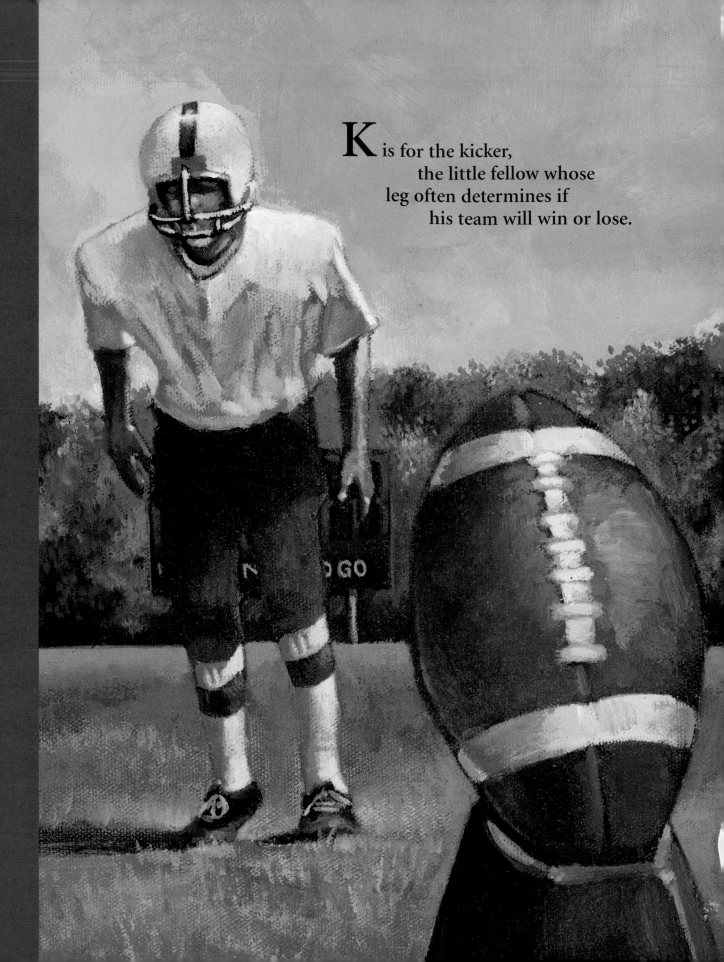

K is for the kicker,
the little fellow whose
leg often determines if
his team will win or lose.

A team's placekicker is responsible for booting field goals, which are worth three points. A field goal attempt usually occurs on fourth down, after a team has moved the ball deep into its opponent's territory but has failed to reach the end zone. The kicker boots the ball from about eight yards behind the line of scrimmage. Usually he approaches the ball from a few steps back and a few steps to the side, a method known as soccer-style kicking.

Kickers are also responsible for kickoffs, which take place at the beginning of each half and after an opponent's touchdown or field goal. The kickoff is from the kicking team's 30-yard line in the pros, the 35-yard line in college, and the 40-yard line in high school. A kickoff returner may run the kick back, but if it travels beyond the end zone it is ruled a touchback. The receiving team then starts its offense from the 20-yard line.

At the start of each play the offense and defense face each other along the line of scrimmage, an imaginary line that marks the spot where the last play ended. The offensive and defensive linemen—usually the biggest players on the team—stare into each other's eyes. They wait impatiently and then rush toward each other as soon as the ball is snapped. It is a great struggle and perhaps the most intense part of football.

Two more **L**s are Lehigh and Lafayette, the universities with the most-played rivalry in college football. The schools had faced each other 139 times through the 2003 season. There are many famous and exciting college rivalries, including Michigan vs. Ohio State, Oklahoma vs. Nebraska, Alabama vs. Auburn, Army vs. Navy, and Harvard vs. Yale.

L is also for lateral, which is any pass that is not a forward pass. Any runner can make a backward pass to a teammate at any time.

L is the line of scrimmage,
where the ball is placed,
and linemen who line up there,
staring face-to-face.

Marching bands put on exciting halftime shows at many high school and college football games. Bands will often play victory songs after games, too. But on November 20, 1982, during a game between Stanford University and the University of California, the Stanford band took the field a bit too early. The result was the wackiest play in football history. Stanford led California 20-19 with just four seconds remaining in the game. But then a miracle happened. A California player received a kickoff and tossed a lateral to a teammate, who tossed it to another teammate... and then another... and another. By now the Stanford band, ignoring the action, began to march onto the field. But after a few more laterals, the original California kickoff returner dodged a handful of band members and rumbled into the end zone, where he crashed into a trombone player. Final score: Cal 25, Stanford 20.

M is for a marching band—
     snare drums and saxophones,
clarinets and trumpets,
          tubas and trombones.

M
m

The University of Notre Dame, a relatively small college in South Bend, Indiana, is famous for its Golden Dome and its football team. The Notre Dame Fighting Irish, as the team is called, have won more national championships (13 since 1919) and have produced more Heisman Trophy winners (7) than any other major college football program. Appropriately, South Bend is also home to the College Football Hall of Fame.

The National Football League is another important **N**. The NFL is divided into two conferences—the National Football Conference (NFC) and the American Football Conference (AFC). Each consists of 16 teams divided into four divisions—North, South, East, and West. The four division winners and two wild-card teams (second-place finishers with the best record) make the playoffs.

N is also for football players' colorful nicknames, such as Elroy "Crazy Legs" Hirsch, Ed "Too Tall" Jones, Jack "Hacksaw" Reynolds, William "The Fridge" Perry, "Neon" Deion Sanders, and "Mean" Joe Greene.

No college team has ever had as much success and fame as football's famous fighting N– noble Notre Dame.

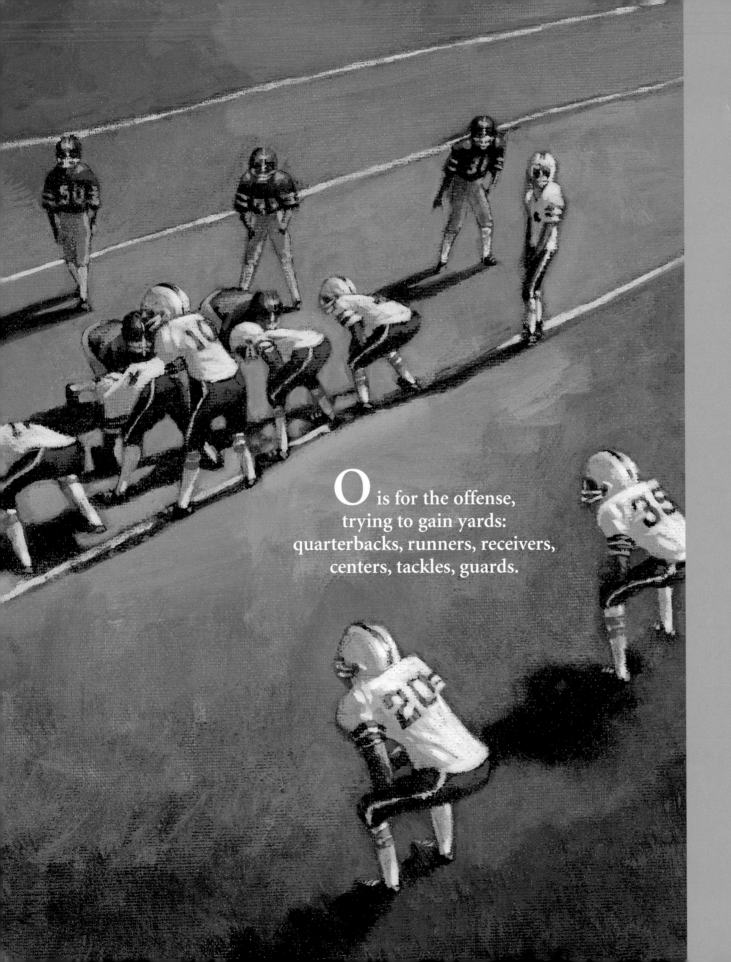

O is for the offense,
trying to gain yards:
quarterbacks, runners, receivers,
centers, tackles, guards.

The offensive team includes the offensive linemen, backfield, and receivers. The linemen (centers, tackles, and guards) block on every play, trying to prevent the defense from tackling the ball carrier. The backfield consists of the quarterback, as well as running backs (a fast halfback and a blocking fullback) who stand behind him. Receivers are the speedy pass-catchers who stand along the line of scrimmage a few yards away from the linemen. A tight end is a blocker who also can catch passes.

O is also for overtime. Pro and college football games are 60 minutes long (divided into four 15-minute quarters). High school games last 48 minutes (four 12-minute quarters). Youth football games are usually slightly shorter. When a game is tied after regulation play, it goes into overtime. In the NFL, the first team to score wins. In most other leagues, each team starts from the opposing 25-yard line, and the team scoring the most points is the winner.

P is for a perfect punt
kicked high up in the air
and a brave punt returner
who tries to catch it fair.

If the offense chooses to punt the ball on fourth down, two important people enter the game—the punter and a center known as the long snapper. The center snaps the ball to the punter, who stands about 15 yards back. He punts it by dropping the ball and kicking it before it touches the ground. The average kick by a pro punter travels 40 to 45 yards. The opposing team's punt returner receives the ball. He may run with it, or he may call for a fair catch, meaning he isn't allowed to run with it and can't be touched.

P is also for Punt, Pass & Kick,™ an annual competition between kids aged 8 to 15. Boys and girls compete separately against kids in their age group. Each participant is allowed one punt, one pass, and one kick. Scores are based on both distance and accuracy. There are local, sectional, and national winners.

Q

Q stands for the one and only
crafty quarterback,
who ducks and darts so quickly
to avoid a sack.

As the leader of the offense, the quarterback uses his arm, his legs, and his brain. In the huddle before a play begins, he tells his teammates which play they will run. Sometimes, after looking at the defense, he will signal a change in the play before the ball is snapped. This is called an audible. He then either runs with the ball, hands it off to a running back or passes it to a receiver who has run a specific pass pattern. A forward pass must be thrown from behind the line of scrimmage. In a matter of seconds, the quarterback must consider where he wants to throw the ball, where the defenders are, and how much time he has before the defensive linemen reach him. If the pass is caught by a receiver, it is a completed pass. If not, it is incomplete. If the quarterback is tackled behind the line of scrimmage, it is called a sack.

In December and early January many college football teams are invited to play postseason games in distant places. These are called bowl games. The Rose Bowl has been played in Pasadena, California, since 1902. It is the oldest major bowl game, which is why it is called the "Granddaddy of Them All." The Rose Parade, held every New Year's Day, is even 12 years older than the game. Millions of people watch the parade on television, and some of the elaborate and flower-filled floats take an entire year to construct.

In the 1929 Rose Bowl, another **R**—Ray Reigels of the University of California—carned some unwanted fame. He became known as "Wrong Way" Reigels when he returned a fumble all the way to the one-yard line—in the wrong direction!

R is also for remarkable receiver Jerry Rice, who is the only professional football player in history with at least 1,500 catches, 20,000 receiving yards, and 200 touchdowns.

R r

R is for the Rose Bowl,
a bowl game that stands tall.
It's the oldest postseason contest—
"Granddaddy of Them All."

S is Super Sunday
            and the splendid Super Bowl,
when two strong squads square off
            with all their heart and soul.

The Super Bowl is the NFL championship game between the winners of the National Football Conference and the American Football Conference. The Green Bay Packers won the first Super Bowl on January 15, 1967. But in recent years the game almost always has taken place on the last Sunday in January, which is known as Super Sunday. It is always one of the most watched television events of the year.

Lamar Hunt, the longtime owner of the Kansas City Chiefs, named the Super Bowl after his children's favorite toy—the Super Ball. Each game is numbered with Roman numerals (X equals 10, V equals 5, I equals 1). So the 38th Super Bowl, for instance, was known as Super Bowl XXXVIII. The Dallas Cowboys and San Francisco 49ers have won five Super Bowls apiece.

S is also for safety. The defense earns a safety (worth two points) by tackling a ball carrier in his own end zone.

S s

The tackle—using the hands and arms to bring the ball carrier down to the ground—is the basic element of defense. But a touchdown is the goal of every football offense. It is scored by running or passing the ball across the opponent's goal line. The defense can also score a touchdown by returning a turnover (a fumble or interception) into the end zone. Touchdowns are worth six points.

T is also for three-point stance, the crouching stance most players take before the ball is snapped. They touch the ground at three points—with two feet and one hand.

The greatest star in football's early years was another **T**—Jim Thorpe. The Native American super-athlete was a college football All-American at the Carlisle Indian School in Pennsylvania, a two-time Olympic gold medalist in track and field, a major league baseball player, and the first man elected to the Pro Football Hall of Fame.

T must stand for touchdown—
six points on the board.
Someone missed a tackle.
That's why the player scored.

T t

Johnny Unitas was a Hall of Fame quarter-back who was famous for wearing a crew cut and black high-top shoes. He spent 18 seasons in the NFL, the first 17 of them with the Baltimore Colts. Unitas led the Colts to three championships and was named Player of the Year three times. He retired in 1973 with more passing yards (40,239) and touchdown passes (290) than any other quarterback. Unitas also holds a record that still stands: He threw a touchdown pass in 47 straight games.

U is also for upset, which is when an underdog team defeats a favored opponent. Perhaps the most famous upset in NFL history occurred in the third Super Bowl (Super Bowl III) on January 12, 1969. Johnny U's Colts were expected to beat the New York Jets by two or three touchdowns that day. But New York quarterback Joe Namath guaranteed a victory, and the Jets won 16-7!

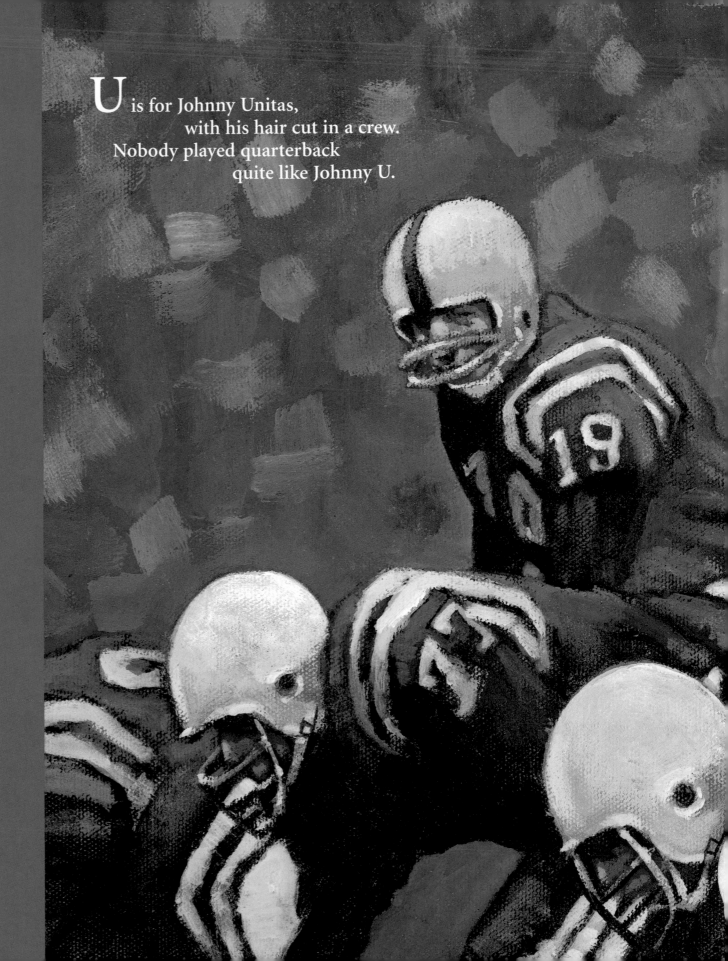

U is for Johnny Unitas,
    with his hair cut in a crew.
Nobody played quarterback
    quite like Johnny U.

V

V is Vince Lombardi,
the head coach in Green Bay.
"Winning isn't everything.
It's the only thing," he'd say.

Although winning isn't everything (all-out effort and good sportsmanship are more important), Vince Lombardi was known for his dedication to achieving victory. In his nine seasons as head coach of the Green Bay Packers, Lombardi led the team to five NFL championships, including victories in the first two Super Bowls in 1967 and 1968. His coaching record has never been equaled. Since 1971, the winner of the Super Bowl has been awarded the Vince Lombardi Trophy.

The head coach is the person in charge, but he will often be assisted by an offensive coordinator and a defensive coordinator. Major football programs also have coaches for each position on the field, such as an offensive line coach, a quarterback coach, and a special teams coach. Special teams players are the athletes who take the field when their team kicks or punts the ball.

The Pop Warner Little Scholars™ football program, named after legendary college coach Glenn "Pop" Warner, began in 1929 with four teams in Philadelphia, Pennsylvania. Today, it includes more than 6,000 tackle football teams, 900 flag football teams, and almost 5,000 cheer and dance squads for kids ages 5-16. Safety is an important part of Pop Warner™ football. Players are matched up by age and weight levels, and there are strict rules about equipment. Schoolwork is also a focus. In fact, individual awards are presented only for excellence in the classroom. Hundreds of Pop Warner™ players have gone on to star in the NFL, including all-time greats such as Joe Montana, Steve Young, John Elway, and Emmitt Smith.

Football isn't only for boys and men. Many girls and women over the years have competed on high school and even some college teams. **W** is also for the Women's Professional Football League, a tackle football league that began in 2000.

W is wide-eyed kids
who play Pop Warner™ ball
and will their teams to victory
as summer turns to fall.

Football is perhaps the most challenging sport to coach. In fact, some professional teams have playbooks (books explaining the team's running and passing plays) that are hundreds of pages long. The players must memorize the playbook so they know what to do when a quarterback calls the play, which sometimes have incredibly complicated names like "Split right, X drag, Y corner, Z streak, rollout." When a play is diagrammed (designed on paper or on a chalkboard), the letter O usually represents offensive players, and X is used for defensive players.

Each different play requires specific offensive players to run or block in a certain direction, whether it's a double reverse, a draw play, a screen pass, or a quarterback sneak. Defenses have set plays as well. A blitz, for instance, is when linebackers and defensive backs charge across the line of scrimmage right when the ball is snapped, hoping to tackle the quarterback before he can pass the ball.

X is a letter coaches use
to diagram a play.
O is for the offense.
It's always done that way.

Y is many years ago
at Yale University,
when a man named Walter Camp
showed what the game could be.

Yy

A game in New Jersey between Princeton University and Rutgers University on November 6, 1869, is considered the first organized American football game. But it was more like soccer. Players could only advance the ball by kicking or heading it, and the final score was 6-4 (Rutgers won). The person most responsible for taking this game and turning it into modern football was Walter Camp.

Camp is often called the "Father of American Football." As a player and coach at Yale University in Connecticut from 1876 to 1910, he introduced some of the most important rules and changes in the game. He is responsible for the scrimmage, which made football different from soccer and rugby by giving one team undisputed possession of the ball at the start of every play. To prevent one team from controlling the ball for the entire contest, Camp proposed the down system, which requires teams to move the ball forward 10 yards or lose possession.

Z is for the zebra stripes
worn by referees,
who call it as they see it,
including penalties.

Football referees have often been called zebras because of their black-and-white striped shirts. Seven officials work a typical game. The head linesman stands on the sideline, marks where the ball is placed, and keeps track of the downs and yards needed for a first down. The line judge stands on the opposite sideline and keeps the official time. The field judge, side judge, and back judge stand downfield and watch for penalties on pass plays. The umpire stands five yards behind the defensive line and watches for scrimmage line violations. The final authority on the rules is the referee, who stands 10 yards behind the quarterback.

An official calls a penalty, such as holding or pass interference, by throwing a yellow cloth flag. The penalty is then revealed through specific hand signals from the referee. The other team may accept or decline it, and the penalized squad is usually punished with a loss of yardage or a loss of down.

Zz

Brad Herzog

Brad Herzog's first job as a newspaper sports reporter allowed him to travel with the Cornell University football team. He has been writing about the game ever since. A past Grand Gold Medal Award winner from the Council for Advancement and Support of Education, Brad has written more than a dozen fiction and nonfiction children's books, including two others for Sleeping Bear Press—*K is for Kick: A Soccer Alphabet* and *H is for Home Run: A Baseball Alphabet*.

Brad is also the author of *The Sports 100*, which ranks the 100 most important people in U.S. sports history. His first travel narrative, *States of Mind*, was chosen as one of the 10 outstanding books from independent publishers in 1999. His second American travelogue, *Small World*, was published in 2004. Brad lives on California's Monterey Peninsula.

Mark Braught

Mark Braught's 25 years of professional experience have earned him prestigious awards from the American Advertising Federation (ADDY), *Communication Arts*, the NY Art Directors Club, and the Society of Illustrators among others. He received his degree in graphic design from Indiana State University, and attended the Minneapolis College of Art & Design. He lives in Commerce, Georgia, with his wife Laura, their five cats, and Charlie the dog.

He also illustrated *P is for Peach: A Georgia Alphabet* and *Cosmo's Moon*, both published by Sleeping Bear Press.